# Black Hero
# The Mixtape

*to Nina: Thank*

JACOB MAYBERRY

*For your Dope Spirit*
*and awesomeness.*
*You are helping Support*
*my Dreams*

# Table of Contents

## Hero     4

Librarian Tears     5
Open letter to Luke Skywalker     8
Taraji     10
He fights monsters     13
The Hijab     15
In the time of butterflies     18
When leaping off couches     20
The Purpose Of Her     21
Stream of Thought for those we've lost     24
The last Hero     26

## Villains     27

Untitled     28
The Red Hood     30
Lights Cameras Abuse     31
Batman privilege     32
I gave you power pt.2     34
Vampires Among Us     37
Privilege Malfunction     39
100 Black Coffins     40
Outfits     41
Crumbling Bricks     43

## Life as a Hero     45

Baltimore Boy     46
Love: A slasher film     48
Unemployed Superhero     50
One Punch Man     53
Blurred Vision     56
Padded Rooms     59
The Bezerker Jean     63
Cypher God or
(How I survived high school)     64
Black Superman     66
Class Clown     69
Barry, Alan     74
God has come     77

# Heroes

## Librarian Tears

Ms. Frasier is not your everyday librarian.
In high school she made books into healers.
My 9th grade year I was jumped at a pep rally,
my clothes set on fire in the locker room,
and my heart broken like promises
I would go to the library for a shoulder
and she would exchange my tears for tales
told her I felt like an outsider
so she handed me to outsiders
tale of boys looking for acceptance in a neighborhood of
monsters trying to be men.
couldn't tell you if this was a book or a manuscript of my life
that I never wrote

For 4 years with books we fought tears fast forward years later
she's my co-worker.
In her files she has a mountain of my emotions.
The poems I wrote in high school sit in her cabinet one day she
proclaims they will be worth money and she'll be regarded as
the innovator of the next Shakespeare.
thought I'd be a bard
in a leotard.

As an educator working under the pressure of a curriculum that
turns kids more walking dead than scholars
I can feel the weight of withheld wisdom
Ms. Frasier tells me a Greek mythology story. When the world
was heavy on the back of a god atlas shrugged to strengthen his
positioning

so I strengthen my disposition
even when I'm not proud of this position.

I and this librarian trading words
she's my vocabulary mother.
has children of her own
grown, loves them with all pride no prejudice
she loves them with the force of heaven when she speaks about
them you can compare a cloud atlas to her smile
but sometimes,
the raven of death gleams over every house of dreams.

Her son suffered from depression, his mind a crucible of
thoughts he couldn't escape.
too often the looking glass of our own sadness is too thick to
see through
in this battle for emotional freedom he fell to revolutionary
suicide
I would then see Ms. Frasier's heart inherit the wind,

I watched mother goose turn to the queen of the damned
couldn't help but to think why are we damned,
to be integers in the devil's arithmetic
death has a way of not just making mice of men but making
empty encyclopedias of their love ones

because what do you know?!
when all the facts of your world burn under the Fahrenheit of
over 451 lost happy memories.

How do you remove the Andromeda strain of sorrow from her
veins?
when she cries tears fall in a crippled rhythm like there's a
broken song behind her eyelids.

1000 collected poems don't have the words to relieve her
perhaps I do.

Perhaps in the most important time I can give her words for
warmth
I can tell Ms. Frasier that we have always been a tale of 2 cities
and when I was at my low you pulled this rumble fish from a
pond before drowning under sadness
and brought his heart to Atlantis

I the broken horse of a boy could never have been a black
beauty had I not been sheltered in her womb of words.
the temple of books I prayed to in high school was as precious
as gold

I can never be your son but you have been as good as a mother
to me as my own so I can at least give you my words, my
shoulder, and my love we are library flowers, and the perks of
that, is knowing there is someone who can read your soul

## Open letter to Luke Skywalker

Luke, does living on Tatooine without a father remind you that in a galaxy far away there are ghettos full of children who do the same. Luke do you ever wonder if they are jedis to?

Does just knowing that robots are around you help you feel better about a mechanical existence of growing up on a farm dreaming of the stars sitting beside you?

what is it like to hold a lightsabre? Because when darkness is so close to your life I imagine that type of light is blinding. Luke, what is it like to find out the people who want freedom as bad as you do are criminals? do you relate to the irony of flying solo your whole life only to partner up of with two men who embody that ideal?

Luke, when you save the princess are you saving yourself as well? does it help wash away the memory of the burnt bodies of your ancestors when you know you are doing something to honor them? Luke, when you watch the closest thing you had to a father die could you ever imagine the possibility that it was by the hands of one that forgot to show you that love is a death star that will often block your view of the constellation of hope?

Luke, like you many of us have found homes in the belly of the beast, in the cold kiss of an Arctic I love you shaped like the Grim Reaper on your face. Luke, when you find your travels have taken you to a dark place does it help to close your eyes and move with your mind when the world around you has left you paralysed? does it help to know that there's a force that can remove doubts from your mind because there is no amount of midichlorians to wash away a history pain.

Luke, when you had your moment in the sky and found out that you had a father did it hurt that the only hand he ever gave you was a mockery of the one he just took away from you? like all the hands He never pushed your bikes with as a child, like the hand that never raised you as a child.

Luke, is falling away from him the closest to suicide you could get before you realize that there is no escaping being a bastard in the afterlife, I think you have enough ghosts visiting you to remind you that there is no death only repetition.

Luke, does Carbonite freeze the nightmares as well, because if so everyone should pretend they owe the huts. Luke, stop imagining a world where little teddy bears run around freely, it it's a false premonition of the childhood you didn't have. Luke, is finding out you have a sister the greatest news in the world because now you know you have someone who cares if you die or the worst because you are stuck in a cycle of men who don't recognize their family when they look them in the eyes.

Luke, did you know a Sith is just someone who felt the force of love and turned away from it. Luke, the dark side is just an accumulation of memories in a life of being unwanted. Luke, stop looking for your father what's left him burnt away on the ashes in a volcano of your mother's tears years ago, the disfigured man you stare at is a crippled reflection of yourself.

Don't you know the law is that jedis are not allowed to have children because holding a baby in the same hand you hold your lightsaber seems like blasphemy to some. Luke, when he drops the closest thing he has to father, know this is where the cycle ends, your name is Sky Walker that does not mean you are meant to take a leap. celebrate Luke, you didn't become him.

## Taraji

She has thunder in her thighs
God behind her eyes
and when she walks she walks with pride
this black Adonis
born goddess, in the flesh
beautiful mind beautiful body and yes I'm talking about Taraji
P. Henson every Wednesday she makes my flat screens

levitate with her high functioning intellect and looks,
got a n**** hooked on primetime television
did I tell you I have visions,
of her visiting me at night and me screaming Yvette!
I'll be Jody, me and Tyreese are the same complexion
so me and this baby girl can make a baby boy.
Taraji you know what I really like, other than when you told
Derek Luke come get this cookie,
I loved how good you made motherhood look,
I like the way you wear being black like a fashion statement,
because it is.
I Love the way male patriarchal culture is your nemesis.
Taraji you are blessed black woman, because you never make
your curves more important than your character even when
playing a character.
When I think of a black woman
I think of a house built with brick and encased in steel,
I think of Joan of arc and how fire couldn't have killed no sister
when I know there are African women who give birth in 80
degree weather,
I think of Oshoun,
I think of the opening of do the right thing,
I love that sweat, love

10

that hard work aroma,
behind every strong woman is a man who wants to be as
strong, but fails in comparison
it's embarrassing how easily black woman handle the hard
times,
the world on our shoulder sounds dumb when these sister's
wear the galaxy as their ear rings,
Taraji you are apart of a long lineage of black icons,
you got that Clair Huxtable class
and both aunt Vivs' swag,
got that Whitley Gilbert appeal,
now I know why this earth don't know how to treat our
sisters...it's a different world where you come from.
You don't need to be nobody's basketball wife, When you are
the love in Hip-Hop,
ever wonder why rappers talk about woman so much? it's
because they pretend that Mic is an umbilical cord and they're
trying to get back their connection to their mothers back,
keep calling you bitch because they can only wish for
something as loyal as you,
Even in your menstrual time
you're divine,
blood don't stop your grind
you got a Hustle in your flow,
Taraji you're an empress and This planet is your entire Empire,
black woman you are empresses and this whole planet is your
Empire.
So third rock that shit girl,
from the sun cuz you're the ones
who set our Son's on the right path, y'all got that Harriet

Tubman loving inside you is freedom,
I want your revolution,
Taraji you are Olivia pope dope,
your physique is Cleopatra stature, your spines
design
aligns
with pyramids, I want your Gina, want your Tina, want your
Oprah, want your Mya, want your fire I want your Hara. most
of all Taraji I want your strength,
I see that thunder in your thighs
God behind your eyes
and when you walk you walk with pride because you are
black
woman.

## He Kills Monsters

Somewhere in a high school not so far away there's this kid, he's about as cool as a thousand bee stings. But every day after school he goes home, changes his outfit and he, kills monsters.

When playing Dungeons and Dragons you get to create your own characters, uses his real life to inspire some of the adventurers and the monsters he will run into. At the end of the quest is a castle that holds, his self-worth.

There's a dragon, the Face resembles that of his mother's. She smokes enough to actually be mistaken for one. All her hateful words burn him so she does breathe fire while he holds his breath.

The next big creature is an invisible man so it's hard for me to tell you who he looks like but I know, that the boy doesn't see his father much and the only way to stop the invisible man is to make him see you so I have a hint of who it might be.

There are these vicious demons who have laughs that can cripple the strongest of men, they can weaken you just by pointing their fingers. These demons, they look like cheerleaders, They cast the word faggot like a spell let me tell you he wants to come out of the closet but the skeletons that await him on the outside are more horrifying then anything in there.

Everyone in his game is gay every creature, fairy, every elf, every warrior and if that sounds wrong to you, a world full of gay people then ask yourself why? This boy just wants to use his pair of dice to live in paradise, because when he's not rolling them he wants to die. It's one of those lonely nights, and for the first time he's drinking he has just done gin because he hasn't mastered how to get over his pain. He is ready to take his life. He never did complete the quest to find his self-worth, just like we never acknowledge the bodies of the bullied until they become a hashtag. To his friends he will be remembered as he who killed monsters. But the ones in his head... were unbeatable.

## The Hijab

I've confused a lot of things in my life. but never could I
mistake a hijab for a Cape.
until I saw Her, like a comic book written in a high school
hallway
her name is Nora, a Muslim girl,
her eyes did something that would make sunlight jealous
she moved like time was waiting on her I would see her and
glance
not stare, I was afraid if I looked too long I would break like
most men made of glass when a woman of steel walks by,
some days she would look back
we'd connect eyes like her pupils were buttons and my irises
were shirt loops. And I would look to the floor,
where people like me belonged.
In High School I was a cliché story,
a narrative of nerdom.
my nerves were made of nitro-glycerine, I would explode from
fear
if she ever got near.
one day in the library,
when I was buried under A tombstone of literature
I saw her without her hijab; For one week Nora didn't wear it
and I saw her hair it was fire red,
I began thinking how does she rest in bed when she could burn
everything she lays on, and as if out of a high school movie,
she sat next to me.
said "Hey"
I replied as cool as possible and said "that's for horses"
ok not so cool but then she laughed,
let her face shape into a moment

into a memory, I still see that smile sometimes when I close my
eyes.
I asked her what happened to her hijab. In my 17 year old
ignorance I commented "doesn't that anger your God".
"She told me I don't think he'll mind for a week "
I try not to speak.
I'm practicing living in this miracle minute
Because I know when it's finished
I'll wish I was still in it

For the first time in my life, me and my words had a personal
scrimmage
the image,
of a girl this beautiful
was unusual
not that I hadn't seen my share High School beauties but this
was my high school movie
and I'm no Freddie Prinze Jr.
I know nothing of pretty in pink but I know that in that light
blue skirt she looked like a summer sky.
I knew her brown hands could henna tattoo a poem in my
larynx.
That I could recite in Arabic,
I Knew Scripture was a physical being when I touched her face
I've never felt more holy than the moment she read eyes like a
Quran. lightly brushed her face against mine, she didn't kiss
me
She saw my Superman chain.
the one I wore like Medal of Honor, thought it was fitting
seeing that she had gripped my heart so tight that it turned
purple.
She asked me if she could wear it for a week like a new hijab,
like

16

that Superman "S' was a new faith in God and she did it
I would sometimes wait in the hallway all day
to see her walk by with that chain on. For a week that chain
was her help to escape "S" around her neck  complimented her
red hair that flowed like a Kryptonian cape
it's funny really,
you'd think a comic book nerd would know when he was
looking at a superhero but hijabs make for a great disguise,
now whenever I think of Heroes
Nora is in mind.
With and without her hijab.

## In the time of butterflies

My grandmother has a shattered Chrysalis.
My mother has been a caterpillar for too many years.
My great Grandmother was a butterfly,
And she flew for years.

Like Faith gave her wings.
When she passed all butterflies in the kingdom came to mourn.
She was a queen butterfly.
Her womb
was responsible for about 95% of the room.
My Grandmother won't get out her limo,
She spent the whole week of her mother's passing re-growing
her chrysalis.

They came to get my mother,
she is the strongest caterpillar on earth.
Though she was never a butterfly
She gave birth to two, who went through no chrysalis phase
they were just butterflies.
Like it was nothing else they could ever be,
Like from birth they were meant to fly.
My mother goes to the limo, and for the first time in my 26
years of life
I see her chrysalis grow.
She screams "Margaret Anne!! Jeanette would not like this" My
Grandmother Wales.
Not in the face of death
it was just hard for her to face the death
Of her mother.
My mother pulls her out of the limo with all the strength

of the human spirit.
My Grandmother Screams at my mother " That's My Mother

in there!!!"
My mother screams back "Then you go get her!!!"
"You tell her you love her!!"
My mother is pulling a bolder
My mother shrugs with the world on her shoulders my
grandmother is experiencing levitation,
Her chrysalis cracked
She grew wings.
My mother is pushing a thousand pounds of pain.
Her chrysalis cracked
She grew wings.
They arrive at the casket.
The room has fluttered to the ceiling.
My Grandmother is the oldest of 13
This is the first time they've seen her
Fly.
My mother is the oldest of three
This is the first time they've seen her
Fly.
When my  great grandmother's years of flight ended I never
thought my family would see flight again.
But amen
With her end
she was able to mend,
my mother and grandmother's broken wings
And I learned that love can never die.
Learned that at a funeral, life was in supply
I realized
I
Live in the time
Of butterflies.

## When leaping off couches

As a child,

Imagination suggests

That any blanket, shirt, or bathroom towel can be a cape.

When leaping off couches,

You must accept this.

The distance from the couch to floor is more than just flying;

It's a leap of faith.

A kiss blown towards danger.

A levitation on carpets.

A dance with air that you don't have to know the steps to

I would leap off the steps too.

My fingertips gently nailing the railing

Damn near impaling my chin on the landing.

This would be my routine spanning through elementary but I never got hurt.

I was always caught,

By a man made of steel.

His arms blessed with fatherhood delivered me safely to my feet.

I would eventually stop wearing capes,

These days the couch I leap off of is cushioned with depression

And I'm always so desperately trying to stay on the steps to success, afraid to move.

Even still

In the midst of broken will

My father remains the voice and the hands of healing

My father, never traded in his cape

I learned from him how long one can be a super hero

I remind myself,

When leaping off couches

Whether because you're a hero or doubt your ability to be one

It's best to remember that they're hands just shaky as yours waiting to catch you

And being a hero can be as simple as helping someone fly.

You master flight by seeing what an angel looks like.

So when you're ready to be a guardian, even if for no one but yourself

Buy a couch,

How  can you train heroes without it.

**The Purpose of her**

She wears scars like linen

She speak poems like Lennon

She break dance on struggle like a cardboard box

She juggles vengeance and forgiveness

Ain't no clown though.

She balanced adversity and jazz in the same hand

In the other

She holds the birth of man and the curse of Uncle Sam

She a lounge singer,

With the note to every gospel song and Negro spiritual
mastered

She a wind,

She can hurricane hymns into a Klansman's front yard

She can deliver an Amistad from the jaws of a middles passage

She a C section

On oppression

Cuts turmoil out of the womb that birthed it

She a dance move

She a rhythm of liberation

She a middle finger

She the 13th apostle who don't give up her seat for whites

She a poem,

She super strength summoned through stanzas

She a 64 impala

She cruise on the face of injustice

Her name is freedom

Her purpose is that of warrior,

Armed with her we fight,

Her purpose is to be sword

Is to be lion

Is to be dragon

Is to be marches

Is to be sung

Is to be shouted

Is to be heard.

## Stream of Thought for those we've lost

There is a river in which all life flows.
it is made up of memories. Memories like, the first time you
held him.
when you were his personal photosynthesis.
Any mother will tell you it takes sun rays to raise a son with the
right amount of warmth
and you are burning star.
and you have known Eclipse.
watched darkness in 3D.
felt it in your stomach like love butterflies gone wrong.
death feels like a breakup but broken things are supposed to be
fixed,
like old sayings of stones and sticks,
caskets have a way of being bricks in the ocean, they stay
there.
but the beautiful thing about a brick in the ocean is all the
things that it can see,
in the sea.
there are many things on earth that we can be, but in death we
are formless. Imagine being rebirthed in a world with no war
No scars or sores
where the pain you have endured,
never existed.
I'm not speaking of heaven.
I'm speaking of a dream state.
a place where levitation isn't a miracle. where the clouds are
lyrical.
I'm not being spiritual,
you don't have to be religious to know when someone dreams
long enough they will find a peace,

and I don't need metaphors to tell you there will be grief
there will be good byes
and sorrow filled cries
but there is also a place where the children fly.
they will see you
they will see mountains
they will see valleys
they will see a river
for which in all life flows
where souls go to glow
and where the reflection of your loved ones is seen whenever
you look in the water.
And to see them all you need to do is look back, to let them
know that they are gone but will never leave your stream,
of thought.

## The last Hero

Call her,
"The Spirit Awakener"
She brought an ambition out of me that I didn't know existed.

Call her,
"The Seeker"
She found a man out of a lump of masquerading coal.

Call her,
"Ms. Revolution"
She fights like a boxer for every cause she believe in.

Call her,
"The Back Bone"
She'll hold you up even when she can't stand your ass.

Call her,
"Never Ending Pocket Woman"
She will dig until the lint in her jeans is solid gold if you needed
it

She be something so super she wears her cape on your heart.

She is the woman who loved me.
and that last proof I have that heroes are real.

# Villains

## Untitled

Death ain't no easy feat to come back from.
It took lots of practice.
I remember a time when they tried to bury me under peace but that shit don't work.

I'm a tomb of evil resurrection. I survived in the chamber of police guns and I breathe through Republican speeches. I'm heinous, a pain in your anus.
ain't nothing worse than looking out your window and seeing me stare back at you like a crack induced starlight, like Satan gotta grudge written in the clouds.

I want to work my way in your system, your body and its functions. Then, I want to work my way into your system your political parties and their functions. I want to give your election an erection, because voters go hard when they know their candidate speaks for them. I want to iron your Klansmen hood. I want to shape the lessons in fatherhood so you can spread me to your son. I'm not the disease I'm the cure. cancer with a purpose. My black heart fighting with your white blood cells is the closest I get to desegregation.

This is more like a societal blood clot, stop your blood clot crying, I'll leave your blood clots frying. Like cholesterol, souls I collect them all. you don't even know I'm in you, your mind might as well be a vacant vacation home and I'm the squatter. Done made hell hotter. Been to Harlem and I'm a globetrotter. I caused riots, I'm a survivor.
You can Peep me hidden in police attack dog saliva.
BITE ME!
chew on my rotten core. Enjoy feasting on my rotten food for thought.

28

Racism,
it ain't just in your mind it's in your blood stream, it's in your heart, it's a love thing. And you know what they say about love... it's eternal.

## The Red Hood

In this Red Hood.
The streets is paved with niggas Robbing,
Mobbin,
Goons sharing needles with the goblins.
Bullet dodging,
And still it's the cops that's the problem.
Heard you can swallow death without chewing on this block.
Heard in the winter they can ice skate on your frozen tears on this block.
This the Red Hood
Where your birth certificate comes attached with your Obituary.
Where your parents ejaculate embalming fluid.
Round here, you get running for your life for breakfast, Break Fast or watch death catch up to you because of the speed you couldn't muster.
Where they sell the children for crack because it's easier to raise a pipe than to raise a child.
In this hood we liquify the dead into half and halfs it's called the carryout for reason. We make women twerk that rapture, that ass is going to be the death of you.
In this red hood we know the grim reaper as reflection welcome to the collection of lost souls. We motor bike you to mass incarceration.
This, is the Disney Land for the demented.
This is the Red Hood

## Lights Cameras Abuse

She was built like a Barbie on acid
like, a polluted river, like a fireman's burnt coat, like a pound of
wet coke in a drug dealer's hand, her transactions would mean
pain, like PTSD became a person, like a toothpick with a
purpose, like a rainbow that knew it was a frown, like a crack
house that Jesus visits, like a partnership between a maggot and
a corpse like nails, sweating from waiting for the hammer, like
an inappropriate joke at a funeral like ... Hurt... Like she, was a
model. forced to remodel her face and body to walk a runway
when really she was a runaway hitting the stage, after being hit
in her teenage years she was bomb, in not just her photos she
was an explosion, a grenade with high heels that never seem to
heal. She walked the stage because the walk through hell, was
much hotter.

## Batman privilege

Batman Privilege is the knowledge that the police won't stop you because your symbol and theirs are concomitant

Batman Privilege is being white and knowing you still have claim over darkness. Even though you weren't born from it, just born to own it.

Batman privilege is watching your America run wild with a psychotic smile destroying everything around you.
Batman privilege is you pretending this isn't just your reflection.

Is the cops caring about the Caucasian bodies gone cold in the alley, where do the black bodies rot in the streets of Gotham?

Is my soul seeing so many dark nights that I don't know the difference between my heroes and my nightmares.

Batman privilege is the space between my hood and a mansion outside of the city.

Batman privilege is a cave filled with secrets that can be kept while mine are plastered on the 6 o'clock news every night.

Is running the streets in a suit the same color as me but knowing you're good because the color under your suit is the acceptable one. Don't you notice, you can't see anything on Batman's body but the color of his face.

Batman privilege is the butler that will have to clean up my father's ashes. Is the investigation after the shooting. Is a bullet that reads my death matters

Batman privilege is being able to order millions of dollars worth of weaponry without question, is knowing you can throw batarangs and never be shot, because they don't look like skittles.

Batman privilege is the relief that when I'm killed the media will Harvey dent my memory.
Absolve me of my past sins. As long as I was an important politician / murderer. Batman privilege is those two terms being synonymous.

Batman privilege is the bane of existence, breaking my back for minimum wage when there are those who could travel across the world and become martial arts masters because they're bored.

Batman privilege is money,
is power,
is a golden belt with the answers all your problems,
is a Kryptonite bank account,
is America's finest human beings

Batman privilege is the 1% Almighty unstoppable,
unbeatable,
inhuman.

## I gave you power pt.2

From the God of war to all my believers, behold the second coming.
I was born 4 pounds 7 inches my age be jumping from 9 to 38 to 45 to 357 I be Mr. Magnum.
Daddy named me colt so you could worship me
I'm God!
Even when I get fired I'm on my job.

My anatomy is tragedy.
Triggers be my scrotum, squeeze me and watch how I bus.
I'm an artist of massacre,
when I paint a church mass occurs.
I draw, masterpieces of blood.
The peacemaker that stops your pacemaker.
I'm equipped
with these clips
and each clip
is an eclipse look how I took your son out.
I was never meant for the land of the living, I was at the side of the Grim Reaper for when shit got real made to mock Jesus
I'm Bethlehem steel leave you still I'm Ill.

Took out your Kings.
Turned your I have a dream into screams.
Call me Mr. Gun.
Elimination,
Desegregation, black white I kill them all I'm a chamber Holocaust.
Divine Lord of Columbine.

Back in the Old West they used to call me Smith and Wes, I can make you famous.

Took more headshots than photographers.
Bet you didn't know guns could have an ego, my nickname is
eagle I soar leave you sore bet you miss the time of the sword?
I'm not so personal, I get you from a distance like a
touchdown, get touched you down catching bullets is a lot like
catching bullets.
Bullets be my saliva, I spit a round Watch it Circle around your
intestines molesting your internal organs, you ever had me
inside you?
I can impregnate the dirt with bodies. Don't take my word for
it.
I get endorsements from movies, rappers, cartoons etc.
Children like Chief Keef adlibbing the sounds that's going to
kill him
Bang!
Bang!!
I used to keep track of all the humans I homicide, until I lost
count at infinity.  I know recently I took this little girl, tore
through her lungs until her mouth became a volcano of
sanguine fluid.
If you saw her from the side, you'd swear her mouth was
blooming roses.
I told you I'm an artist.
I'm an apocalypse.
I'm an end.
But I'm also your friend I push movements and revolutions I'm
human evolution the second Big Bang!
You'll never put me down you'd drop your religion first.
The instrument of war but I'm also the piece for peace.
Those who never held me could never know of my affection.
I'm the Messiah hidden under gunfire. Coming to a ghetto,

a Serengeti,
a battlefield,
a playground,
a schoolyard near you.
I'm on tour, silently providing the end of society, why talk out
your problems when I have such loaded conversations!
I'll be here when the roaches are left to inhabit.
Clutched in the hands of the last man who went out shooting.
Everything you enjoy I helped you attain. I'm your freedom
and your chains.
I gave you power, or the illusion of it so hold me, your God
likes to know he's loved.
Show praise,
to the pistol.

## Vampires Among Us

Warning! if you are afraid of horror movies or the truth please close the book.

I love horror movies vampires being my favorite genre.
Dracula, The Lost Boys, I can watch Blade From Dusk Till Dawn

but never ask me if I think vampires are real, because they are.
I've seen them.
I've seen nightmares walk up and down Edmondson Avenue,
Watched the undead Congregate in front of churches, sounds
crazy I know, until you realize how long these young bloods
been killing for blood money trying to prove who's the True
Blood.

Or worse than that, when one of your family members turns in
front of you I watched my uncle Glen
Drugged up,
stagger towards the bathroom mirror searching for his
reflection it wasn't there. When you are an addict the only thing
you can reflect back is your nothing.

My friend Brandon has been an addict for years, watched his
family's tears turn holy water it only burns him to see people
watching his transformation. We want to hold him, bring him
back to the land of living but vampires don't like the site of
crucifixes, so he only rejects us when we try to put our arms
across him

My cousin Shanita, 7 children, divine number.
Suffered from the worst case of vampirism I'd ever seen, she
used to look at her dealers like victims, told them for a hit...
she would suck them, didn't pay much attention to her kids

never looked them in the eyes, it would have burned her to ashes if

she had to see her sons light.
When she died of AIDS I had all the proof I needed that vampires were real, it was one of the symptoms, every time she opened her mouth I could see her coffin

Addiction isn't science fiction, drugs have a supernatural hold on our people and isn't it a curse? Do they not seem to live forever? Post-apocalyptic portraits of a past frozen in pain, it's not an act addict is not a roll that people are meant to play so it's no casting when I say this life will pick you apart

But what role do we play? vampires are not born they are made. they are turned and then turned away from. We'll say how dare they defile their spiritual house but never invite them in to ours.

Isn't it obvious, people bleed you dry because they're not well, so yeah, vampires are real; but the true horror is, if we keep ignoring their existence, doesn't that make us
the monsters

## Privilege Malfunction

Oh shit, the sweaters are burning,
My ties a noose now.
The golf club's spontaneously combust
My law's my precious laws!
They seem crooked,
They seem like a frowning moon
Who's going to scrub these black souls I've upholstered my
house with?
Where bloods the detergent I scrub my car with.
What will mop the floor clean of the oppressed bones I vomit?

What force in America can save me when privilege,
malfunctions.

## 100 Black Coffins

Mamma had a coffin the pitch of night.

Told me that's where I'd end up if I put up a fight.

Daddy had a coffin and 3 graves, different sizes.

One for any age I'd die, he wanted no surprises.

A cop showed me a coffin, told me it was mine.

He cracked an evil grin and patted my spine.

I saw 45 coffins on the news today.

Filled with activists, preachers, and children who used to pray.

I saw 10 of my friends enter coffins, straight from the playground.

The drug dealers can't shoot them, so I guess they're safe now.

I saw 20 black coffins on a television show.

Mamma told me it was a glitch, when the media buries your culture's image you're not supposed to know.

I saw 20 black coffins on my classroom wall.

Pictures of dead leaders, did god kill them all?

Did America kill them all?

Did white people kill them all?

Did my people kill them all?

And if there's a rapture, where will we hide

From the sky when 100 black coffins

Fall.

## Outfits

I come out the house in my Black sweat shirt and Black jeans.
Black on Black
On top of my Black and White Jordans call them,
the segregations,
no one notices though.

They just see all this Black and hate it.
I know that the jeans are faded and that sometimes my Blacks
clash that don't make nothing less beautiful.
It doesn't make my outfit less classy, besides all colors clash.

Nobody brings up how white is with everything.
White on Black
White on white
White on Mike Brown
White on Freddy Gray
White seems to clash with any color you put it with.

But when you see white
you see pure like doctor's coats
When you see Black
you see funeral,
See death,
See darkness
Like there isn't a beauty in that darkness

The goth kids wear black and they're the weirdos, the freaks,
the creepy ones.
Black is never attached to anything good.

Meanwhile someone who wears Blue and Black is a hero.
Even when their outfit is covered in Red stains.
They're never dirty.

41

# Black Hero The Mixtape

Never guilty
Never anything but the pure blood of Christ.

Those people who wear Blue and Black carry nothing but
Black accessories that are used for killing,
so isn't it always death involved when it's Blue on Black?

They also hating on the people who wear pink.
Tell me I should hate them too.
That an ensemble so bright should be kept in the dark.
However, I've never been one to tell people what they can
bring out of the closet when the skeletons in mine wear me.
Besides, we all come out the house fully dressed in a myriad of
our insecurities.

They can't help but talk about my Black on Black.
They don't see my wardrobe
they see a war robe.
It doesn't affect me though.
I love my Black outfit,
For everything it is, not for everything you make it seem,
I love every stitch every seam
It's in my genes.

So before you make commentary on my Black on Black,
check what you wear out the house first,
and you'll find.
They're a lot of outfits much
worse than mine.

## Crumbling Bricks

All in all I'm just another brick in the wall.

They burn me, but I'm already fire red. They want to break down my foundations.
When I've built nations.
My hardened clay was forged in the flames of gentrification.

I'm a brick house, the one the pigs worship, so you wolves don't have enough breath to blow me down when they choke it out of you.

I'm paved throughout your cities. Streets of my DNA have mixed with the black blood that's been spilt on it.
You used to love me.

I gave you ground to stand on and surrounded you with warmth, what human ever did that for you?

They put a part of me on 2509 Pennsylvania Avenue.
Called me CVS,
I thought I was making a difference.
but this store was a front.
I could see them suffer
I was leaned on by fiends
Pissed on!
Watched the fights of those pissed off from their surroundings.
I watched these people who own stores
Ignore the bleeding of the needy.
They must think because what they bleed is brick because they're trying to build America with it.

# Black Hero The Mixtape

They made mockery of me. I'm am strong and made to last yet they name a substance of powder that's made to kill after me.


I won't lie I hate them.
I hate the way I have to put my clay next to decay
I pray, for demolition.
How do you expect to have peace in a place where even the sanctuary is suicidal?

When they tore me down, they threw bricks, isn't this what it means to be black?
Being attacked by what's meant to protect you. You'll see how easy it is to crumble after the rumble of oppression. The lower class is out of class and destruction is in session.

When I burned I became famous.
They spoke my name like victim,
like martyr,
now I know how the concrete in Ferguson felt.

The world brought cameras to my viking funeral.
What they called the aftermath of
a riot was confusing to me.
That neighborhood looked like a warzone long before an uprising happened.

They will rebuild me no matter how many times my bricks fall.
But black bodies,
Will keep stacking you're all just bricks in the wall.

# Life As A

# Hero

## Baltimore Boy

In the heart of the heartless.
corner stores of darkness.
street lights that burn the crackpires who roam below.

The weather change, the people don't. Lives get ditched like
prom dates, left on the side of the road 4 people to witness like
circus acts. My city got a death toll so massive that if they all
rose from the grave they could populate a small country; World
War Z is down every street.

We got open cases with
open caskets
but walk around with closed minds. They got a thousand black
men in a prison trying to get free of their own nature. And they
got guns,
and cops got guns,
and they shoot us
and shoot us for shooting off at the mouth,
getting shot in our pride are anger triggers something.

If they made a movie based on what I've seen it would be too
much like Friday the 13th mixed with 300.
So many bodies that they could be seen from space but because
so many of those bodies are black the earth appears to be a
galactic ghetto graveyard.

46

If Black lives matter then why are there so many atoms
and Adams
that aren't functioning.

Why is it that every time I hear a siren I'm reminded that the
Grim Reaper dresses in blue.
I'm reminded that my home is a holocaust, leaving the house
with a certain outfit means I'll get Auschwitzed.
Marvel at me, I am he who is destined for bullet,
I am walking corpse animated through fear,
I am the negro, the Negus and the necro and somehow I find
enough life and my body to be the Nigger.
I am a Baltimore boy praying that I will make it to see myself as
a Baltimore man.
I am a breathing statistic.
I am body 305, trying to survive the mouth of the street,
before it swallows me.

## Love: A slasher film

There's a serious problem with people in slasher movies that we are neglecting to talk about as a society

For instance, if everyone is telling you that Crystal Lake has been abandoned for years because there is a serial killer there, believe them! the mother f***** in the hockey mask is not wearing it for a fashion statement.

If the killer calls and says he's in the house... he's in the house! Running away from the kitchen where all the knives are, probably not the best idea.

When you've been informed by the sheriff of the town that the guy haunting your dreams only exists when you think of him, this is the time to stop thinking of him.

or, when I have turned from the man you once met. My hands that once held you with love, look like claws or sharpen knives time stop thinking of me.

My past relationships have been a Zombieland, and screaming is all I seem to remember between us. For every new girl, There has to be an explanation. someone's got to explain the monster hiding behind the bushes wearing masks that I'm telling everyone else is a smile.

This isn't an easy life, not being able to tell if you are the killer or the one being murdered, there are times, I find myself slow motion walking into situations with women that look like bloody murder before anyone yells it.

I keep forgetting some of the key rules of a horror movie situation, don't have sex, it always dies after that, never say you'll be right back, chances are when one of you leaves, that door is closed, like the healing of an open wound. Never split up, all directions will lead you somewhere scarier than an abandoned Summer camp. It'll lead you to loneliness.

Turn your soul to a blood soaked knife.

Turn your bedroom to a graveyard full of dead memories.

Avoid endings, the plot twist often ends with you killing your own relationship. When you tell her she's cut, it's because she is.

Elm Street is the address of My pillow. So I can only hope the next one, knows who the killer is.

## Unemployed Superhero

Help wanted,
Help needed,
Cape torn,
Nike superhero boots is ripped,
running up and down the strip, I done stopped about a
thousand purses from getting snatched and y'all can even reach
in them.

I've seen murder scenes and
teen robberies but being broke is the most heinous crime there
is,
you can chalk outline my wallet.

There's a hero in your view, you can't tell by my shirt or by my
shoes but I,
was a god in the sky.
never flew over trouble nor danger
but as soon as I ask for a dollar I'm treated like a stranger
whether superhero or villain, poverty will rearrange ya.

You can't be no hero if your pockets are as flat as a sprained
Cape.
In this world you gotta learn there's a difference between
saving and what's in your savings account.

We're like poets,

I've seen these wordsmiths talk pretty little runaways into going
home with poems.
I've seen bedroom ledges that almost became diving boards
become vacant spaces because a poet help them find their
oasis.
I've seen a poetic war against racists, fascist, and sexist still you
get played like your heroism doesn't exist.

I've seen the stage become a bat cave, where humans change
and the weak turn brave but Hey,

you don't care for heroes,
you just like looking at sacrifice from a distance.
You like to know you've been saved without ever
acknowledging the time it takes to put on a costume,

the family that costume takes away from,
the relationship that costume takes away from,

that classroom where they tell you to Clark Kent your abilities
because who the f*** can save a child with a bunch of poems
and soliloquies even when you know it's what these children
need.

A Poet and a superhero have something
In common.

They're both cursed with the powers of purpose

It's those power's
That keep them
Unemployed.

## One Punch Man

Hey yo, you don't want no problems with me, you ain't never been about this life. You done talked too much s*** though. Squad up, do you even know how to throw them hands punk m*********** squad up. Don't look at me like you stupid Donald ball your fists.

Yeah I seen you on TV talking that b******* like I won't f*** you up. Like I won't slap that stupid s*** toupee off your f****** head, what it is dummy. Nuck if you buck get to rich ass stuck. Tell them Tea Party niggas they can sip my piss. You gotta come outside some time and when you do I'm going to Deebo your face with a brick. Catch you on one of your tour stops and run up on you and strike you with a Koran.

Naw yo 2x, he don't know nothing about me, he don't know where the f*** I'm from. You don't know how many white boys done said that same s*** and got slumped. Ain't got dollar to my name but I got a right hook as smooth as a moonwalk. Boy, you ain't nothin. You're a pescatarian, vegetarian, gone vegan, you don't want this beef. I've been playing Mortal Kombat for whole week which is to say, with one punch I can reach into your chest and pull your spine out. Snatch your soul from the ether the moment it tries to climb out.

He don't want none of this West Baltimore, we'll catch the bus to dat, ass. Me and 15 of my niggas hopping off the MTA, sagging jeans, hoodies, and soda cans, it'll look like you getting jumped by the ghosts of Travon Martin.

Imma stomp him until my shoe size gives him PTSD. Imma punch him in his stomach until he throws up civil rights.

His bodyguards can get merked too. Let that nigga try me dog, if he shoots me in a dream he'd better wake up and sprint. Tell Ben Carson sambo ass he better be booking beside you. I ain't ever been to medical school but I promise you these mits are surgical. I'll knock his fucking heart loose not that he has one any way.

Truth is, I don't even like this country and you might be only a tad bit worse than those who came before you. But you smell like world war 3, you look like a Holocaust, you sound like Hitler on repeat  Zighow You going to see me son. If you even make it close to the White House lights out. In This right hand I got a thousand transgenders in the pinky, I got a thousand Muslim women in the ring finger, I got a million border crossing Mexicans in my middle finger, Che Guevara, Pancho Villa, and El Chappo included.

I got a million gays from my index finger to my thumb. They sit on my knuckles waiting for this hand of fate to seal yours. I'm a one Punch man, I'm going to punch you so hard, that the particles of hatred are going to fly out of your saliva. I'm going to tattoo a bruise that says immigration under your left eye. You don't want these problems, you don't want this punch, I don't want your presidency, I don't want your prejudice.

You not about this life, all I need is one punch, one Punch, ooooooh, just one Punch, One punch.

## Blurred Vision

In December 1975, a 13 year old girl and her mother have a 7 mile walk with a cart filled with Christmas presents.
When I was an alcoholic I never had blurred vision. Whether on the dance floor having to be picked up from a drunken split, Or running from the front of the bar to the back, I never hit a wall. My grandfather in his years of being an alcoholic has hit many walls, and people.
I guess that's his way of showing affection.

This little girl and her mother walk the carts filled with gifts through seven miles no matter how cold it is they make this journey.

never saw my grandfather get up early for church, don't think he ever went, but I know I've seen him in the morning getting up for work and to drink, thought that was his job
knew that's what he worshiped so he didn't need God

called my brother white boy,
called my cousin Cortina princess,
but called me monster.

I'm in the room drinking casually by myself.
knew it was out of depression,
knew I couldn't pull myself out of that Jack Daniels and I pulled for days.
knew I was yelling at Nakia,

seen myself zapping out over a bottle of liquor but couldn't stop.

felt like I was justified, like that bottle was my just deserve, like I just deserved a drink before I go to sleep.

Before I wake up

Before I go out.

This woman and her daughter are pushing this Kart a 7 mile walk through crackheads, thieves, and many other horrors that the Baltimore Streets can offer and their father was too alcoholic to bother.

Didn't know I was an alcoholic just figured I'd like drinking, never thinking that this has become the best parts of my year. Could have told you I wasn't that guy.

could've wrote you an essay on the terrors of ingesting liquid death corroding my inside but it started to feel good, tasted better than my own name,

looked better than my reflection.

My grandfather used to clutch those 40 bottles of Cobra like someone having a heart attack clutches their chest. Like he thought it was going to run out, like he had ran out on his family. Remember my grandmother sending me down to

Lexington Market to go get him off his bottle, I see the weak I need help out of bathtub of a man that he is now and the irony that my grandmother takes care of him.

I'm afraid that the only people that will take care of me is my demons. My grandfather used to make my mother and grandmother walk for seven miles with Christmas gifts cuz he was too drunk to do anything but hate himself into whiskey. I've never had anything in common with him, it kills me that the first thing that makes us family is our addiction.

The first sign that me and him are alike is the amount of times we don't care about our loved ones more than a drink. How my grandmother saw his filth in my eyes when I stumbled in the house drunk.

I haven't been drinking in months, kicked it out of my life like an abusive lover because that's what it

I now walk 7 miles of depression because of the destruction I have done to my life alone with nothing but my presents.

my grandfather used to call my brother white boy used to call my cousin Cortina princess and called me monster, who knew it was because he saw his self in me,

alcoholism runs in my family I just pray that I'm faster. I could always see clearly when I was drunk, had no idea I was seeing my life, through blurred vision.

## Padded Rooms

Padded rooms are a trick.
Soft surroundings
While you're going through hardships.
Staying sane is some hard shit.

To Kray, my student.
Don't let them call you crazy, even if it's a clever play on your
name.
Even after you went to Sheppard Pratt
There is respect in that.
They give medals to people who survive wars even if those
wars are in your mind.

The truth is I hear voices too, they tell me to rhyme
And they tell you to perform.
To form words of wisdom
These words you dance with them
Like spoken word is an exercise and your demons are fit.

I do not subscribe,
To doctors telling lies about what mentally unstable means.
If you could have read my dreams
As a teen
I would've made Charles Manson's house look like the playboy
mansions.

Thoughts full of rabid horrors and shattered karma.

As a youth I wouldn't kill myself, because I had poetry.
As a man, as lonely as a single tree in a burnt down forest
The only reason I'm still breathing is my students.
Watching your spoken word movement
Is why there is movement in my bones.

When they told me where you were
I felt a hurricane in my heart.
Saved myself with this art
Never thought that it couldn't save you too.
Never knew the pain couldn't be written out
Like an exorcism with ink.
I couldn't imagine that the devil is a better poet than me!
And I've lost a child before, to neglectfulness of my youth

I won't lose my student to the voices she can slam louder than.
I'm sorry I'm no Rebecca Dupas, with the ability to save
classrooms with poetry.
Every day I walk through the doors of a school and slam for
the souls of teenagers.

I will not let Kray Romeo and Juliet her stress
Won't live in a world where they call her crazy.

Crazy is a curriculum with more pressure than drowning lungs,

Crazy is crying every day, cake dry tears on your face and
people only noticing your mascara is smeared.

You know your god is a poet as well?
I hear he writes poems to forget people in hell

He wrote one poem and put it in the sky
Billions of lights illuminating the darkness in a universe, a verse
for uni (You and I)
And you and I will always confront our discomfort.

Demons don't die, they get recycled
In the cycle of life.
We are not strangers on the boulevard of broken dreams,
Reach out your hand and I will catch you.

Off the trapeze trap called living.
Your mother told me
That poetry was possibly what's been saving your life,
But sometimes spoken words go silent.
Art was still there for Cobain
And he still had to blow his brains to find nirvana.

In life we need people to remind us to be straight jackets
Holding yourself makes you realize that it's not so bad to be in
your flesh.
And together we will slam against
The voices, and we will win.

The bond between a teacher and his children is unbeatable
group piece.
I'm no one's father, just a man who cares for my student like a
daughter.
And love, is the only sanity you need

## The Bezerker Jean

As a child, my favorite x man was Wolverine, obviously! Logan had the power to heal from any injury, and he was a bad ass! The mutant version of Clint Eastwood. Talked real gritty, tooth picks and true grit.

Wolverine is often searching for the Truth of his past. A bullet to his skull renders his memories obsolete so Logan just wants to know where he came from. I always knew the X-Men had themes from black culture, but this is as cruel as a joke at a funeral. I know at least a thousand Wolverines, searching for a past that the school system never taught them, perhaps they think if we remember the Bullets we took to the head we will weapon x their school yards.

There is a sadistic irony in a character who cannot die when the country I live in is trying so hard to x my genes out of existence, and the moment we reveal that we have claws that can bring cataclysm to a continent they magnetize our bodies to a graveyard filled with adamantium coffins. Because our death is the only thing that's indestructible.

My new favorite X-Man is Gambit. At least he gets to choose the hand he's dealt but that just means he burns his fate whenever he tries to play his cards right. I know what It means to be Wolverine. I know how to have a metallic heartbeat. But I have yet to figure out how to heal from the wounds of being black.

## Cypher God or
## (How I survived high school)

So I'm walking through the hallways of the high school I used
to attend and now work at and I hear a beat.

Some kids are making one against the lockers while another
one raps and I can feel my spine reverberate.
Cuz I'm a MC.
I turned words into holy water/
blessed like the Holy father/
My bars a shinobe slaughter/
Spitfire and Joan of Arc ya/
every ill line I toss ya/
has Pedigree's higher than Triple H attending Harvard/
I come around to wear their cypher is going on and they know
Mr. Jacob.

They know the para educator who rap's. They expect me to
drop some bars but I don't, I walk past their cypher and nod
my head. After school one of them comes and asks me why
didn't I spit?
I wanted to tell him.

I wanted to tell him that when I was in high school I got to be
The Cypher God, through words I learned to decipher God. I
want to tell him that at his age I was more rhyme book than
human being, that those hallways were my stage,
That I walked around with hoodie on, headphones blaring

whole school staring
Spent not one second caring
about anything that anyone thought.

I was all base no stereo,
all Busta Rhymes what's the scenario! so what's so what's the
scenario! Drowning out the weed smoke that had lungs
collapsing.
Drowning out math, I was done with fractions.
every time I turn on the news, something happened.
One of my classmates dead from the guns they clapping.
I was Rah! Rah!!
Like a dungeon dragon.
Back when my depression was dumped and dragged in.
Even when I was at lunch with mad friends.

I wanted to tell him that he looked like salvation.
That him and his friends reminded me of walking through the
hallways not going mental because I had a instrumental.
Not shooting up the school because the voices in my head
wear beats.
Not shooting myself because I knew my life was a lengthy lyric.

I wanted to tell him that I hope hip hop can save you too.
Instead I told him... the beat was whack.

## Black Superman

Levitating over the globe I be a broken star.
shattered over this tenebrific world below, I be atheist God
my self-hate is stronger than a speeding locomotive
I've seen souls leap from project buildings in a single drop
who fears suicide when in the projects home looks a lot like
hell
and who's going to save you?
I know!
it'll be me
it'll be Black Superman
I'll use my super strength to reshape the Statue of Liberty into
Coretta Scott
I'll play all sports at all times
go down as the greatest of all time black people, with me you
don't have to worry about dying
it's only the symbols who get shot.
it's hard to be faster than a speeding bullet when they seek out
melanin. obsidian bodies crack like levees when hit
and justice... seems to never league with my skin,
because it's okay to be a hero when you fly high or courts and
move fast through fields
because America likes to move you through federal courts and
hang you high over fields.
trying to be black and Messiah
you'll find your churches on fire
The media will turn your Martin Luther into Lex Luthor.
burn your image so much that seeing yourself is like having
heat vision.
it's hard to make new heroes when crooked ideals are what they

base their life on
their moral high ground looks like a burned down Gotham
and this "s" stands for streets
stands for strength
stands for stolen
stand struggle
stands for sorrow suffocating sons so severely something
snaps
This ain't no red cape I got on my back.
this is a blanket soaked in the blood of BLACK children
I have tried to be there when the world is in its lowest Lane
and every time they
end my time.
I had a dream once,
left it splattered on a balcony
That moment when you don't know if this poem is about black
Superman or MLK's ghost
the answer/
both

because whenever there's a black hero the outcome
is Malcolm
X marks the spot where you get shot .

Do you know what they call a black man who wears a

costume?... nigger
you know what you call a black man who works to change
things?... Dead nigger
be careful if you want to be Superman,

they will put you in a crypt tonight

and your soul will meet with the others who died in your cause
and they will float,
levitating over the globe
you'll be broken stars,
a once Guiding Light shattered over this tenebrific world
I be an atheist God
because it's death
to believe you can be black and a Savior
so when I ask myself,
can I be the martyr or wear the mask of Martin
that attracts bullets like magnetism. Could I sacrifice
be cast as Christ
just to be praised in my afterlife longevity has its place...but let
me tell you,
To know death is certain and still be willing to step in front of
the target
and free my people from hardship that's how heroes are made
that's what black Superman does
So I choose, death because the alternative is silence, that ain't
living

## Class Clown

I don't think they'll ever call me a hero

BUT I WAS!

In theater I was the entertainment and the teacher

I held the whole class's attention

Did I mention

That I would sometimes stand on top the desk and dance like James Brown

For no other reason than wanting to get on up.

I once punched myself in the nuts to make this girl stop crying

I'm not lying, in high school if I saw a tall ladder and a good place to land

There was going to be a diving elbow

I was the Jeff Hardy of the party

Living in a lifetime of laughter

Because I knew after the school bell rung

I was going home

to my thoughts.

Believe me when I tell you it's not always healthy to be alone

with those.

I was never tested for A.D.D.

But just sitting for me

is impossibility

I need to watch movies

Write lyrics

Write poems

Learn lyrics read comics

Because somewhere within the silence in my solitude.

Is a voice that yells from my loneliness,

It says things like who loves you?

It mumbles I love yous that aren't there.

This poem is for all the teenagers who know what it means to
be a class clown

because if you're giving everyone a show

your true face won't show.

People won't see that you think this life is god's prank

I'm not dancing in the middle of the hallway because it's fun

I'm trying to see what enjoyment looks like on everyone else's face so I could mimic it.

I knew back in high school that I couldn't have been the only kid walking around with a costume

Of happiness topped off with a red nose.

So I was dancing for them too.

Have you ever seen the movie It?

There's a part where the evil pennywise stops looking like a clown

And shows his true monster form

The only difference between me and him

Is I wasn't written by Stephen King.

So I would laugh

and laugh

And make others laugh

Until I could learn to do it

By myself.

I've made people laugh my whole life

Because when I was younger I learned that people need a break

between the moments where they could break

and making people smile in a classroom can feel like a trophy

that no one can see or know

that they gave you.

The trick is...

You can't make people laugh if they know they're all in on the joke.

Like waking up every day,

It's got to be a surprise.

They'll never call us class clowns heroes

But trust me when I tell you

You're saving lives every day,

Starting

With your own.

**Barry, Alan**

What if I told you

    when I see you

       I begin to understand The Flash

          That when you are around my
      heart beats 10x

         faster than the

         speed of light

       I know what it's like to

    run…

     love can be as fast

  as frightening

 as a speeding
bullet

*and*

I'm not bulletproof

          there is a

lightning bolt in

my chest

from the countless

women

   that left burn marks on my heart       like
a signature

my silent screams

could break the sound barrier

I can make a sonic boom out any woman

I attach myself

to

my blood is r  u  n  n  i  n  g

so fast

my cells could vibrate

out of my skin

with one touch

you will go ~~right through me~~

75

I am
　　ghost
　　　　a
　　　　decaying
　　　　version
　　　　of the
　　　　man I
　　　　was

too fast

for wind, time & gravity

I knew what it meant to be caught

held

in her arms

there are
nights

where I, Jacob Alan　　　　want to Barry Allen

strip out of this speed suit and

lay against *you*

like a normal man

but　　　　　　　I'm still running　　　from the
memory of her

**God has come**
wearing a hoodie that says black lives matter on the front and
on the back,
a picture of Jesus to say,
we will always hurt what loves us, like ourselves.

God has come,
putting his finger into malt liquor and turning it into self love.

God has come, holding both the world you live in and the
world you think you live in.

God is here, and the horrors I've seen were a test,
preparation to be in the presence.

God was never in your Gucci bag or your Lui bag, he was in
that fight you had.

He was in that knife that tiptoed across your throat instead of
slicing

He was in that grin you kept ziplocked.

What if I told you God was standing beside you? like a divine
shadow and the chills you get down your spine was him telling
you he's got your back.

What if God was that kid with the Dre beats, nodding his head
to heaven with dreams to slay beats.

## Black Hero The Mixtape

What if God was in every kiss, because love like God is
something you must feel.

What if I told you he was a riot, why else do we call it an
uprising but why do I say these things? what literals have I seen
to scribe these visuals?

I saw God on North Avenue.
I'm staring at the street, trying to play Superman in traffic,
praying that I wouldn't be faster than a speeding car because
I've had prayers unanswered for so long,
like they got his ears and crumbled like burning houses

when I went to take my leap of hate
it was the leap of faith.

I couldn't move.
My tears we're runaway children finding a home.

My feet became as heavy as a crucifix on the back of a profit
and when they could move, my shoes become Jerusalem.

Something saw my pain and sorrow and stopped my suicide so
God has come!
from a literal crossroads.

Though he didn't evict the demons he taught me to make them
pay rent, because what is hell when you stand next to flames.

I now see, how people misuse their Messiah, I've seen people
piss on Eden.

Turn technology into idolatry, what did you think you were

doing when you picked that Apple phone?

But I'm not talking about religion.
God is in our decisions,
you wake up and see him or her every morning.

My experience taught me that God exists in the moments you
realize He exists in you.

I'm a God fearing man because I fear the God I could be.
Forgot about the God that was inside me.

Didn't realize every time I spit rhymes I'm walking on flows.
I crystallize concepts in to red words my God words be a Bible
for black survival.
I teach kids to use their poetic prophecies,
put Psalms in their palms
let my Mohamed's build A Mecca
God has come,
Showed me I'm worth a second chance
Showed me I'm worth his greatness.
When God show's you your purpose
You've got to prove you're worth it.
I've learned, theirs a miracle on every mile
And if you walk it, you might find wing's on your shoulder,
a halo in your pocket.
God is in everything.
But that divine light is at the end of a tunnel of your darkness
God has come
He whispered in my ear,
You're not done

Made in the USA
Columbia, SC
19 January 2019